Foreword

Anyone who has lived has probably experienced at least one scenario that left them with conflicting emotions. In general, most of my memories from the last twenty years of my life have left me with thoughts and feelings that can often be contradictory at times. What is contained in this book is neither an endorsement or an attack on the topics that I grapple with, but are just that, perceptions and emotions that are at war within my head. Therefore, my work should be viewed as just that, me battling my demons and wading through twenty years of repressed and often confused mental and emotional states in an artistic manner. With that in mind, please enjoy.

Sincerely,

Michael Hyde

Table of Contents

Revolutionaries

Load your guns, ring the bell boys
Revolution is on the way.
Rome may not have been built quickly
But it could crumble in a day.

Talk is cheap, words can be easily ignored.
Violence spreads, destruction sends
A signal pounding down the door.

Yet the counter culture siren
Has gone strangely quiet.
Weaken the voice of the alternative youth
The message dies when society buys it.

Water down the passion, monetize the look
Chains, spikes, and vulgar words
No longer leave the elders shook.

So saddle up the sinners
The skeptics, and the saints
Tell the world to be prepared
Revolution's on its way

Perhaps in order to fix something,
Something has to break.
Maybe the world will be prepared
When the future is at stake.

Wise Too Late

I am a child, performing in hope of
receiving tawdry trinkets.
This duplicitous existence convincing me
That the cheapest of pleasures
Are worth my highest efforts.

Satisfied for but a moment,
I pour out my all.
Only to return again and again
To receive the same substances
That previously have left me unfulfilled.

Foolishly, I pursue that empty thrill
Wasting away beneath a weight
That by its nature, is self-imposed.
Soon, I have nothing left to offer.

Having had its way with me,
The world throws me away,
Like a infant who has tired of her dolls,
And leaves me to die.

Used up, I accept my fate
Mourning as I watch those younger than I
Take me for a fool, mocking my words

And unknowingly stepping into the snare
That will claim their lives, as it did mine.

The Value of Tears

What if every painful thought, feeling and
fear
The terrible words we say to ourselves, and
Each of the hurtful things that we hear
Were trapped deep within our soul
And could only escape if it were a tear?

Unreleased emotion, the weight of our own
sorrow
all of the unfulfilled dreams of tomorrow
Leaving us feeling broken and hollow

Would freedom not be within our grasp if
we
Could swallow our pride,
Instead of further pushing sadness deep
down inside?

We choose instead the empty smile that
Will lead us to our deaths
Our weary souls, no longer heavy
Will be finally at rest.

But alas, what a legacy after us
Could have long survived

If we had not sacrificed our joy
And allowed ourselves to cry.

After a Fight

If each word I've written here
Was a brick, then all i would have built
Is a wall to further separate
Us from each other.

The sum of my good intentions
Not enough to repair
The ropes supporting the bridge
Spanning the chasm between us.

And so, I'm left alone again.
Reduced to a whimpering child
Shivering in the corner
Bowed beneath the weight of the pain
That I tried so hard not to cause you.

<u>Codependent</u>

I awake each morning to a sense of dread
Billowing around my mind
Fogging the surface of clarity like steam
Clouds the mirror after a hot shower.
The whispy tendrils of sadness
Assure me that today, everything
will go wrong
Sucking the very hope of a new day from
my soul
Like roots greedily depleting the ground of
nutrients
as they entrench themselves in the soil.

So long have these thoughts been my
Most dependable companions that
I could not imagine my existence without
them.
To rid myself of their company is a thought
that leaves me
Feeling empty and alone.

Afraid to face a life without my
Most constant of comrades,
I travel on.
Hating their deplorable company,

But never quite hating them enough to
entertain the idea
of sojourning forth on my own.

Addiction

I may feel every emotion in the world
tonight
A cacophony of sensations swirling around
in my head
Frantically attempting to brush them away
and out of sight
Like the things that I keep hidden and swept
under the bed

The burning flame of unquenched desire
Matched only by sickening revulsion
The ceaseless push and tug
A love that I hate, and hatefully love
Reduced to the whims of my latest
compulsion.

Caught between who I am
And the person I wish to be.
Tho perhaps I am the one who forged these
chains,
I am too sick to set myself free.

Help me. The cavernous hole in my soul
Is drawing me in, I'm not in control.
Scared, that this time I could die

But all you had to offer was judgement
That burned from your eyes.

Mom, I'm okay. It's me, I'm fine
But mother can't hear me because I've
crossed the line.
Everyone is crying, why did he not seek
help?
There was no one who wouldn't cast
judgement,
Not even myself.

Alienation

I feel empty and incomplete
An existence coldly surreal.
Like a shadow floating through a world of
the concrete,
An abstract replica of something real.

My song is flat and hollow
Each note distorted and garbled,
As if hearing it underwater or
In a far off dream.

Is this my lot? To be forever a
Shade of grey in a world of color
A cloud of isolation and despair
Impenetrable by the light?

No, for I am only lost and alienated
As defined by those who belong.
Worthless by their measure,
But perhaps their measure's wrong.

Physician, Heal Thyself

Judge, jury, hangman all present
"Tell me, how will you plead?"
The answer is bitter upon the tongue
For myself, I cannot deceive.

In silence I stand, while my case is carefully
considered
The judge stands to speak,
the crowd looks on
My sentence is solemnly delivered.

Ashamed of my guilt, I stand condemned
The noose tightening around my neck
A life wasted removing logs from others'
eyes
While blind to my own speck.

Absolution

The endless void rapidly expanding
inside the hollow of my my chest
Ceaseless voices in my mind
that never seem to rest

Each weighty failure causing pain,
keeping me awake
Pangs of guilt pierce the heart
With every breath I take.

My soul's fabric starts to tear
It's substance long wearing thin.
It seems my soul's search for exoneration
Was doomed to be over before it could
begin.

Can my depravity be remedied
And I too far gone to save?
Is there a way to be cleansed,
Or is my fate bound to the grave?

Perfection, far beyond mortal reach
For in sin we are conceived
A single transgression meaning that
The Law has been irreparably breached.

Fallen by nature, unholy
Unable to perform restitution
A consummate sacrifice must be made
if I am to obtain absolution.

A Prayer for Redemption

This treacherous road has been hard
Saturated with sorrow and pain.
Surely you understand, for you made me
And once dwelt in this fallen domain.

I confess that I have been wayward,
Toiling for a mere taste of worldly delight.
Pursuing treasures that slip through my
hands
That dissipate like a thief in the night.

A sinful and destitute soul long tainted
Having discovered the vapid allure of
pleasure
is more empty than once it seemed
Seeking the light and desperately pleading
"Father let me be redeemed".

For even in my vain wandering
Never have I forgotten your Name
Your Word that I have hid in my heart
In my heart, has always remained.

I long at the end to hear those words,
"Welcome my child, well done".
I beg and I pray, don't turn me away
In spite of who I've become.

Intrusive thoughts

As long as I have remembered
I have had the nagging wish to die.
At least, I thought it was the wish to die.
But perhaps, rather, it is the desire to live
Truly live, beyond this shadow of reality.
To throw off the chains that bind me here
Keeping the infinite just out of reach.
Humanity, a small piece of the eternal
Packaged in fragile mortal shell.
What I perceived to be a curse, perhaps
Is rather a rare and weighty gift.
An ear tuned to pick up the call of the
heavens
Calling me beyond this temporal plane
To the realms of the unknown.

Questions of Juxtaposition

Is order able to be birthed of decay?
Is the existence of night a result of the day?
Is it fair to blame pleasure for the sensation
of pain,
Or to believe water was made to balance the
flame?

Can meaning be found where chance reigns
supreme?
Could a word be created if it conveys what I
mean?
Is a human been, or to be, worth the same as
a being?
Is the weight of the truth truly something
that is freeing?

A question posed, is it a waste if
It lacks an answer?
Is the value found in the dance or the
dancer?
Who can determine what is of value or of
waste?
Is a mark still a mark even once it's been
erased?

Meta reflections

If I could capture this moment,
Pick it up and firmly hold it.
Look at it closely from every side
Would there be something new to find?

Each thought that seemed a waste
Decisions that I have deemed mistakes
From these would precious wisdom pour
Or would I feel more inconsequential than
before?

The risk of assigning value where none is
deserved
Was the agony felt worth the lessons I
learned?
Does the weight of my loss equal that which
I've gained
Is this the life that I chose or the path that
from birth was ordained?

Lie of the temporal

The thought of dying, ever present
Desiring to be free, no longer confined
To this world so sharply defined
By the cage of my senses.

To some, freedom is found in perception
The ability to explore with the mind, a gift.
I, however, understand the deception.
Through embracing the tangible,
We remain enthralled in our bondage.

Blindly infatuated with the temporal,
And oblivious to the evidence of decay.
Time invested in that which cannot last
Only to slip into eternity, empty and
unfulfilled.

Barely Jekyll, Mostly Hyde

I think we all knew it would end this way.
I've always been a little too different,
A stranger to this world
The tension in my soul tearing me apart.
When I cried out for help, I was met
With voices of false bravado
Telling me that "I could do this".
And so I will.
Never realizing the war in my soul,
Only enough to push me away when
The tendrils of my chaos made your life
inconvenient enough to care.
My demons have been in control for too
long.
Having lost ownership with my dignity
All those years ago.
At least mother was kind enough to shove
soap down my throat along with my feces
Cleansing me, killing me, the beautiful
paradox.
I've always been the supportive one.
But as soon as I cry for help, I'm a burden
too heavy for anyone to bear.
I'm not Michael, but a broken shell
A ghost of a sensitive boy scarred beyond

repair,
Always hungering for myself, but lost
Knowledge the only thing coming close to
fulfilling the void within.
And so I crash and burn. Pushing you away
Because it is you I have loved
And I want you safe from the aftermath.
I pray that the explosion is beautiful, and
that
My soul will be cleansed. I pray
The darkness within coalesces with the light
And what will be remembered will be better
than the memory that could have been.
Taking fate into my hands, surrendering
Allowing the demons to remove my last
sliver of control
For by choosing to surrender control , I
know that ultimately I still have it.
The only proof the Michael (or some
semblance of him) remains.
I have lived, I have loved, and I have lost
How much more is there to feel?
The sorrow of my soul far greater than
Any around can seem to comprehend.
So now I wait for the end, alone
That no longer I will be a burden.
Believing that the memory of loving Jekyll

Is best, isolating, because I fear
That only Hyde remains.

The Mark of Cain

I look at the person I could have been
Through the cage in which I am trapped,
The bars made of the cold, solid steel of my
own ignorance.
My intentions were good, naive tho I was
Not that it matters now.
Each choice stacked upon the last
I buried myself, thinking that I was digging
my way out.
Convoluted thoughts coagulated in my brain
Intoxicating me, until I
Exorcised my friends and embraced my
demons
Not knowing who was who, I chose.
Here I am, knowing that it's over.
I gambled, I lost.
My best, not good enough
And I have nobody to blame.
No longer given to the passion of youth
The curse is almost more than I can bear.
Alone in a world built of decay, I wander
Bearing the mark of Cain.

<u>Hypocrite</u>

Where were you
When the only place I could find solace
Was in the embrace of the unholy?
Doers of good, absent in my hour of need
Yet was I welcomed by the sick and the
sinners.

Your self-righteous gaze condemns you.
Lifting a finger to bury the ignorant
But never to help provide relief to the lowly.
Perhaps my hands are unclean,
But my eyes are not blind to your oppression
and deceit

Even if you were holy,
Unstained and pure enough
To cast out my demons
Why would I let you?
At least they were there for me,
Which is more than I could say of you.

So I make my bed among the rejects,
The sinners and the sick.
For in the darkness, somehow have I
Gained a better view of the light.

For bread-crumbs are the scorn of the rich
But to the starving, they are sustenance.
Similarly have the "pure" lost the value of righteousness
But the sick rejoice in even a single drop of goodness.

A Skeptics Prayer

I look up at the expanse of stars
More numerous than the souls here below
And feel the weight of my finite existence
lost
In the meaningless bustle of vapid lives Ever
racing to and fro.

Before i inhaled a single breathe, at best
One hundred years of my time here
remained
With each gasp of air, I am closer to being
laid to rest
The fate of all frail mortals the same

I ponder with great skepticism the Mystery
For many attempt to deceive
Unafraid to cling to faith in the Great Divine
But refusing to trade thought for empty
belief.

God did not grant me inquiry to waste
Blindly following in the steps of those saints
so adored.
The convergence of thought and childlike
faith, I pray

Will take me deeper in experiencing You
than man has ever traveled before.

Seasonal Depression

I watch the autumn leaves erupt with color
Then float gracefully to the ground
Then I hear the rapturous sound
Of the wings of the wind whispering
through now naked tree
Softly crooning " come, my love, find your
rest in me".

I will keep you safe from snow and ice
Provide shelter from blistering cold
Below the earth, your youth preserved
Blessed never to grow old.
Here forever free from all of life's harms
Come, find solace love, resting in death's
arms

And alas, the season changes
All colour now white and grey
Freezing blood, polluting soul and stealing
breath away
A world once ripe with vibrancy conquered
by icy decay

I gaze out the frosted pane
upon the frozen wasteland that

Reflects the pale moon's light
And I hear the reedy voice of the stars
Calling from the night

"The world is cushioned in silence
Except the mournful howling of the breeze
The days frigid, dark, and hard
So come, find your rest in me

Look how all things in nature, have accepted
my embrace
Come out, and allow my bitter breath
To numb your pain and freeze the tears that
grace your face

I will warm you, and your eyes will grow
heavy
Finally you can sleep
Knowing that this rest is final,
Your soul eternally I will keep".

And just when I am about to succumb
As the voices grow ever stronger
I see hints of golden rays of sun and the days
begin growing longer.

The snow slips slowly away
Revealing shoots of green
The birds chirp their welcome to the first
signs of life
That mean the arrival of spring

As each day passes, I feel my spirits rising
And a stirring in my soul
A giddiness, a delightful warmth
That I almost cannot control.

I am safe, and abundantly alive
Free to grow and to thrive
To renew my strength, as I have learned
There is no sense in running.
For like death, I am aware
That the fall is coming.

Time Passed

The charred remains dot the landscape
Gone are the legacies and the names that
those building once contained
And the secrets that only the walls were
allowed to hear.

Here hopes were birthed, and dreams
decayed
Souls escaped while their shells remained
The lives they chose, or were ordained by
fate
Like childhood tears, they are wiped away.

Malleable is the past, shaped by those
Who know the least, and fear the most
History, often story at best
Since we save what we like and discard the
rest.

More Fitting a Farewell

How does one go about saying goodbye
To a life never truly lived?
To say farewell to the hope of the
unattainable "one day"

The days spent here, a blur
A tumultuous river of suffering
We push ever on, believing
That glory will ensue a direct
Result of our pain

Refusing to acknowledge, that truly
We were prisoners of this world
Placed against our will
And unable to return whereabouts from
which we came

Truly, the integrity of the soul will show
That we are "condemned to be free, alone,
And without excuse".
What more fitting a farewell
Than the revealing of the puppet master.

"à tout le monde, à tous mes amis, je vous
aime, je dois partir"

Foster/Adopted

I am a dandelion, planted among the flowers
of the garden.
An outcast, and unwanted.
Unbeknownst to me, and without my
consent,
Was I uprooted, and transplanted
Only for the new gardener to deem me a
weed, and persecute me relentlessly.

So long have I questioned why I felt that I
did not belong,
Never knowing that I was foreign to the soil.
Painfully aware that my blossoms were
unlike the others,
I was afraid to allow myself to grow
And ashamed of my dissimilitude.

Today, I am learning to find pride in my
divergence
To thrive in the midst of a new place.
Knowing that tho some may find only Fault
in my existence,
To the gifted eyes of the innocent,
I am of value.
And am worthy to be allowed to grow.